REAL WORLD ECONOMICS™

How Taxation Works

Laura La Bella

+6.73
+1.33

+21.64
+14.83
+9.19
+3.24
+32.47
+11.02
+2.35
+25.06
+.021
+.242
+5.53

ROSEN PUBLISHING®
New York

Published in 2011 by The Rosen Publishing Group, Inc.
29 East 21st Street, New York, NY 10010

First Edition

Library of Congress Cataloging-in-Publication Data

La Bella, Laura.
How taxation works / Laura La Bella.—1st ed.
    p. cm.—(Real world economics)
Includes bibliographical references and index.
ISBN 978-1-4358-9463-1 (library binding)
1. Taxation—United States—Juvenile literature. I. Title.
HJ2381.L23 2011
336.200973—dc22

                                                                2009047165

Manufactured in the United States of America

CPSIA Compliance Information: Batch #S10YA: For further information, contact Rosen Publishing, New York, New York, at 1-800-237-9932.

On the cover: Form 1040A, the simplified version of Form 1040, is used by U.S. residents to file their income taxes.

Contents

4   Introduction

Chapter One
8   Understanding Taxes

Chapter Two
23   Why We Pay Taxes

Chapter Three
36   The History of Taxes

Chapter Four
47   The Effects of Taxes

Chapter Five
58   The Future of Taxes

67   Glossary

69   For More Information

72   For Further Reading

74   Bibliography

77   Index

INTRODUCTION

W hen you start receiving a paycheck from your first job, it can come as a surprise that you don't get to take home every single cent you earn. In the first paycheck from that fun summer job as a lifeguard, waitress, or employee in a store or amusement park, you might try to calculate how much you'll be receiving by multiplying your salary by the number of hours you work. But when you look at your pay stub, you'll soon learn that you won't bring home every dollar you so carefully calculated. Don't worry. Your employer probably didn't forget to pay you. Instead, you are learning about an important responsibility that comes with having a job: paying taxes.

You probably knew that when people worked, they had to pay taxes. There's no doubt you've heard your parents or grandparents complain about taxes. Your paycheck will show you that if there's one thing you can't escape, it's taxes. Everyone

pays them. No matter how old you are, what you do for a living, or where you live, you will pay taxes.

The most common tax you'll pay is income tax. It's probably one of the easiest to understand, too. When you have a job and you are making money, a portion of your income is withheld to pay taxes. But there are many different types of taxes in the United States. You will pay separate taxes to the federal government and to the state government in which you live. Plus, you'll pay taxes to your local government (the town, city, or county you live in), and you'll pay for services you might not even understand yet, like Social Security and Medicare/Medicaid.

While it can be frustrating to see your hard-earned money go somewhere other than in your pocket, taxation is an important part of our government. The U.S. government acts as a very large business with a lot of debt and expenses.

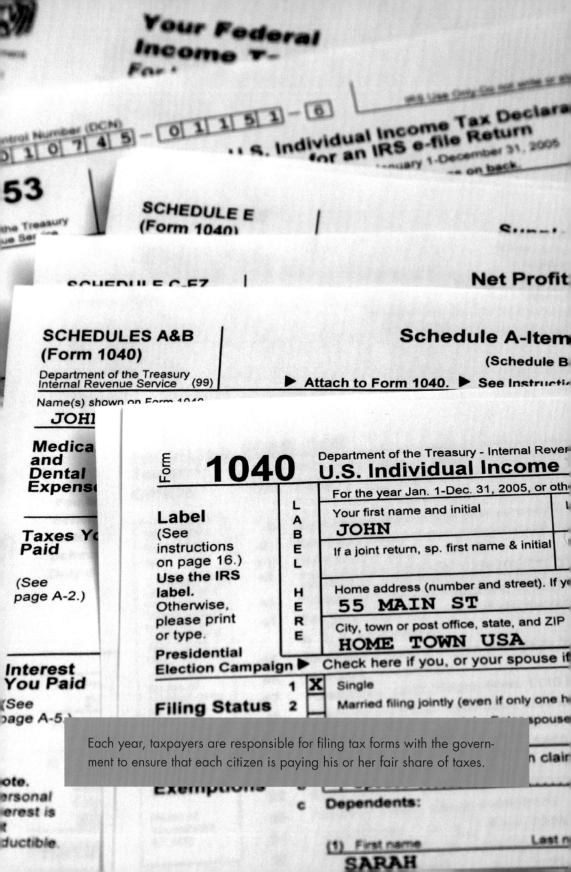

Each year, taxpayers are responsible for filing tax forms with the government to ensure that each citizen is paying his or her fair share of taxes.

Many of those expenses are services that we get to use as citizens of the United States, such as public assistance and education. Other services, like our military, keep our nation safe during times of war and peace. To handle these costs, the government needed to create revenue. Our Founding Fathers created a tax system in which every person in our country contributes money from their income to support our government.

As a U.S. citizen, you'll be paying taxes for your entire life. This book is an excellent place to begin your understanding of how taxes work, what kinds of taxes we pay, why we pay them, where the money goes, and who spends our tax dollars.

CHAPTER ONE
Understanding Taxes

I bet you've heard your parents talk about taxes. You may have even heard politicians talk about raising or lowering taxes. Everyone pays taxes. That's right. Most purchases—whether they're video games, magazines, CDs, or books—are taxed. You might be asking yourself why we pay taxes. How can a few cents added to the purchase of a CD be that important? Learning about taxes and why we pay them is important to understanding how our government works.

In its simplest form, a government determines the way in which a country, state, county, town, city, or village is run. At every level of government, laws are created that citizens must obey. Policies are put in place for just about everything connected with our daily lives. A community—whether that community is a nation, a state, or the town where you live—needs an organized way to function, and a government provides that framework.

The U.S. government provides public goods and services for the citizens of the country as a whole. But since our

In most cases, taxes are added to the cost of an item. This type of tax, called sales tax, helps fund projects in your city or state.

government doesn't generate an income of its own, it needs a way to pay its bills. The money that our government uses to pay these bills comes mostly from taxes.

Taxes have been a part of American history since our earliest days. In fact, taxation forced on the colonists by the British government was one of the reasons the colonists fought for independence in the first place. They drove our nation's founders to declare war on Great Britain. However, when writing our Constitution, the Founding Fathers knew that our young country would need the money generated from taxes to help build streets and roads, buildings and parks, schools, and national defense.

What Are Taxes?

Simply put, our government charges its citizens taxes, which pay for services used by everyone. Taxes pay for services that citizens use in their daily lives, such as the U.S. Postal Service or police protection. They also pay for services that protect our nation as a whole, such as the armed forces, which protect the nation in times of war and peace.

There are two groups that collect taxes: the federal government and the state government. The federal government taxes

Soldiers from all four branches of the U.S. military—Army, Navy, Marines, and Air Force—help protect our nation. Our tax dollars pay their salaries and buy the equipment they need.

people by using a universal chart based on a person's income. The chart is the same no matter which state you live in. States work a little bit differently. Each state government can set the tax rate, or the amount of taxes people pay, and they can differ widely from state to state. Citizens pay state taxes in addition to the taxes they pay to the federal government. The reason for this is that each state offers services that are different from the services offered by the federal government. For example, federal taxes pay for the military when the United States goes to war, but state taxes pay for your local protection, like the city police force and fire department.

Types of Taxes

There are a number of ways our government collects taxes. We pay different types of taxes depending on our income, the kind of purchases we make, and whether we own property or a home. The amount we pay in taxes varies as well. We may pay a higher tax on our income than we do for a clothing purchase at the mall. Among the most common types of taxes Americans pay are income taxes, Social Security taxes, sales taxes, property taxes, and excise taxes.

Income Tax

As its name suggests, income tax is tax that you pay on the money you earn from your job or investments, known as your income. Businesses also pay taxes on the money they make from selling goods and services. This type of income tax is called a corporate tax. Everyone who earns a paycheck pays a federal income tax, and forty-three of our fifty states charge their citizens a state income tax.

Federal income taxes support government programs, such as defense and education. The United States has what is called a progressive tax system. This means that the more money a person makes, the more he or she pays in income taxes. Someone who makes very little money pays a lower tax rate than someone who earns a very high income. Federal tax rates appear in a chart that assigns a tax rate to your income bracket. For example, if you earn between $0 and $8,350, you fall into the 10 percent tax bracket, which means you pay 10 percent of your income.

An income tax bracket is a category based on how much money you make. In 2009 and 2010, there were six different tax brackets with these rates: 10, 15, 25, 28, 33, and 35 percent. Also, your tax amount can be different based on whether you are single, married filing jointly (filing taxes together on one tax form), or married filing separately.

It can be hard to understand how your total taxes are calculated because you actually pay taxes at a given rate only for each dollar that falls within that bracket's range. For example, if you earn $9,350, the first $8,350 will be taxed at the 10 percent rate, but the last $1,000 will be taxed at the 15 percent rate. State income tax works in a similar way.

When you receive a paycheck, you may also pay state taxes on the money you've made. This is in addition to paying the federal income tax. There are only seven states that do not have a state income tax. They are: Alaska, Florida, Nevada, South Dakota, Texas, Washington, and Wyoming. State income taxes are usually much lower than the federal income tax rate.

Some towns and cities also impose local income taxes on their citizens. Again, this tax would be in addition to the federal and state income taxes you might pay. For example, in New York City there is a state income tax of up to 8.14 percent and a city income tax of up to 4 percent. These local income taxes help pay for local services, such as snow removal in the winter, public schools, and police and fire departments.

Social Security Tax

When you review your paycheck, you will see the amount of money you pay toward federal and state taxes listed on the pay stub. You might also see the word "FICA" next to a small amount of money that has also been withheld from your pay. This is the amount of money you pay in Social Security taxes. Also known as the Federal Insurance Contributions Act (FICA) tax, this tax helps fund Social Security.

Social Security refers to a social insurance program that was created by the U.S. government to protect its citizens against the effects of poverty, old age, disability, and unemployment.

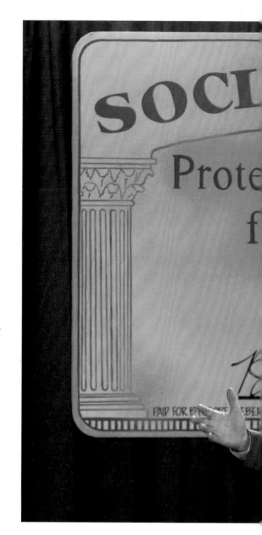

Sales Tax

Local governments impose a sales tax to raise money for local projects, like building schools and libraries, supporting prisons,

As a vice presidential candidate in 2000, Senator Joe Lieberman spoke about the importance of Social Security. Taxes support the Social Security program.

and staffing fire and police departments. The rate varies from county to county and city to city. Sales tax is imposed on items you buy from stores, such as clothing, shoes, furniture, CDs, DVDs, and electronics. Automobiles are also taxed. Food purchases at restaurants are often taxable, but food purchased at a grocery store may be exempt.

Sales tax is called a flat tax, meaning that everyone pays the same amount of tax on an item. This tax is not based on your income. Even if you make more money, you will pay the same amount of tax on a sweater as someone who makes much less money than you do.

Property Tax

Property taxes are taxes that you pay on real estate. Taxes on land, and the buildings on it, are the biggest source of revenue for local governments. The village, town, city, or county where your property is located is in charge of collecting these taxes. Your local government decides the value of your real estate, such as your home, your business, or any other property you might own, and then determines how much money you should pay in property taxes. The money the local government raises is usually used for building schools, building and repairing roads and bridges, and snow removal. Property owners pay property taxes each year.

The owners of homes and land must pay property taxes. The town, city, or village assesses the value of the property and collects a percentage of the value in taxes.

Excise Tax

Excise taxes, also called "sin taxes," are additional taxes people pay for items such as alcohol, tobacco, and gambling. These taxes are put in place to help discourage the purchase of these items or, in the case of gambling, to dissuade certain behaviors. In the case of cigarettes, there is a federal tax of $1.01 added to the price of each pack. People also pay a state tax, which varies depending on where you live. The top five states with the highest state tax on cigarettes are Rhode Island ($3.46), New York ($2.75), New Jersey ($2.70), Hawaii ($2.60), and Wisconsin ($2.52). New York City, the most expensive place in the United States to buy cigarettes, charges an additional city tax on cigarettes. There, an additional $1.50 is added to each pack. Combined, that's $4.25 in taxes (state and city) alone that people pay when buying cigarettes in New York City.

Excise taxes can affect the economy and influence consumer behavior. An excise tax is used to discourage the use of products and services that could pose a risk to someone's health, such as alcohol or tobacco. Luxury taxes are paid on expensive, non-essential items, such as luxury cars. Revenue from luxury taxes is redistributed through government programs that benefit all citizens. Do these taxes discourage the use of unhealthy products or the purchase of expensive items? Some consumers groups say yes, while others argue that no, they don't change behaviors.

Indirect Taxes

Taxes can be either direct or indirect. A direct tax is one that the taxpayer pays directly to the government. These taxes include income tax, Social Security tax, sales tax, property tax, and excise tax. These taxes cannot be shifted to others. An indirect tax is one that is passed on to another person or group. Fuel for our cars is an example of a tax passed on to consumers. The cost of fuel includes a tax that consumers pay, which raises the price of gasoline. Instead of oil companies paying that tax, they pass it on to consumers.

Tax Collection

When you pay taxes, the money goes to two places. The federal government and your state government both collect the

Is Sugar Under Attack?

There's a new tax that makes a lot of people angry. The federal government is beginning to tax beverages that contain excessive amounts of sugar, such as soda, fruit drinks, and sports drinks. The people who work for companies that make these drinks are trying to prevent Congress from passing this new tax. Obesity is a growing health concern, especially among children. This tax would force people to pay extra to buy drinks containing sugar.

Those that support the tax say that drinking sugar-sweetened drinks can lead to obesity, diabetes, and other health ailments. They say the tax would discourage people from buying these items and possibly reduce health problems. The soda industry says that taxes won't help teach children or adults how to make healthy choices.

If this new tax passes, could taxes on other unhealthy items—cookies, candy bars, fast food, potato chips, and ice cream—be next?

taxes they charge on your income or on purchases you make at stores. The money the federal government collects is sent to the Internal Revenue Service (IRS). The IRS is a government agency that is responsible for collecting taxes. These taxes fund

The Internal Revenue Service (IRS) is a U.S. government agency that is in charge of collecting taxes and enforcing the revenue laws. The IRS is part of the U.S. Department of the Treasury.

federal government services, such as the military and homeland security, Social Security, and health care services like Medicare and Medicaid. Taxes also support offices that have certain responsibilities, such as the Department of Education, which

supports student achievement and educational excellence; the Department of Labor, which promotes the American worker; and the Department of Agriculture, which oversees food, food safety, and farming. Additional departments include the Department of Health and Human Services, which protects the health of the American people; the Department of Housing and Urban Development, which educates the public about home ownership; the Environmental Protection Agency (EPA), which helps maintain a healthy environment; and the National Aeronautics and Space Administration (NASA), which researches space and science, as well as many other offices and departments. Running the federal government itself costs money, too. Everyone from the president of the United States to the staffers that work in government

21

agencies are employed by the U.S. government. Their salaries and the costs of running each of these offices are also paid with the taxes collected from citizens.

Most state governments that collect taxes send the money to a taxation department. This office is responsible for collecting taxes and distributing the money to state agencies to be spent on services for the public. State taxes help pay for public schools, police and safety, state-run colleges and universities, statewide roads and highway systems, and health and public services. These services include public assistance (also known as welfare), health programs such as Medicare and Medicaid, and other services that people use directly.

CHAPTER TWO

Why We Pay Taxes

Everyone pays taxes in one form or another. All American workers pay federal income tax, and most states (all but seven) impose state income taxes. We pay taxes to cover the expenses of services offered to us as citizens of this country. These services include federal services, such as Social Security, health care, and national defense. They also include social services like food stamps and housing that our federal income tax contributions help fund. Our state income taxes and local taxes support services such as our public schools and libraries and maintenance on our streets, roads, and highways. They also support health care, prisons, and social services for citizens who have very low incomes or who need special assistance.

Your Role as a Taxpayer

As a taxpayer, you are responsible for paying your taxes and filing a tax return. A tax return is a document that shows the federal and state governments what you are declaring as

By April 15 each year, Americans must complete and submit tax forms to their federal and state governments. These forms show how much each person has earned and how much each person owes in taxes.

taxable. For example, taxable items on your income tax return include your salary, tips, and any income from a house or any property you own, such as rent paid to you. Everyone who earns a certain amount of income must file a federal tax return, which

shows the federal government how much money you have paid in taxes. The federal government then reviews these forms and notifies you if you have paid too much in taxes or not enough. If you paid too much in taxes, you will get money returned to you. This is called a refund. If you have not paid enough, you will be told how much more you need to pay. Filing with states that impose an income tax works in a similar way.

In the United States, all tax forms are due to the federal and state governments by April 15 of each year. Since computers are now used to help calculate tax forms, you can file your forms electronically, which saves time and money. Our nation's tax system is a voluntary system. This means it is each taxpayer's responsibility to report all of his or her income. It is against the law to fail to report your income. It is called tax evasion.

Tax evasion is a serious crime. The IRS estimated that in 2007, Americans who didn't pay their taxes owed more than $345 billion in taxes. This is money that our government loses.

People who do not pay their taxes can be sentenced to one year in prison for each year they avoid paying their taxes.

As a taxpayer, you have responsibilities. These include:

- Knowing when and where to file your tax return.
- Keeping accurate and complete records of your income.
- Giving the government (federal and state) accurate information on your tax returns.

While taxpayers have a responsibility to file an accurate and timely tax return, they also have certain rights that protect them and the personal information they share with the federal and state governments. All taxpayers have the right to privacy of their tax information. Only authorized tax personnel can examine, or audit, a tax return. Even law enforcement agencies have no right to examine a person's tax returns. In addition, taxpayers have the right to appeal any IRS-proposed adjustments to a tax return or contest the results of an audit.

Paying for Use

As you have already read, each person pays taxes for services that are offered by federal, state, and local governments.

The American Recovery and Reinvestment Act of 2009 funded construction projects, education, job creation, housing, and unemployment benefits.

Taxpayers often argue that they pay for services that they rarely use or will never use. We don't just pay for the services we actually use because very few people would have the ability to afford these services.

Think about it like this: If you had to call the police department to report that your car had been stolen, would you be able to afford the police services? What if you had to pay each time you drove your car on your own street? Someone has to maintain the roads, bridges, and streets that we drive on. What about the sewer and water systems in your town? Would you be willing to pay each time you turned on your faucet for a drink of water? If we all had to pay each time we used simple services, we'd never be able to afford to live our everyday lives. With luck, you may never need to call your local police department, but if you ever do, isn't it good to know that you won't be charged a fee to report a crime or have an officer respond to your concerns? We pay for all of these services in the form of taxes so that they are available to society as a whole when needed.

Calculating Taxes

When you understand why people pay taxes, you can see that each citizen is a vital part of society. Now is a great time to learn how all of these different taxes are calculated.

Federal income tax is based on a percentage of your personal income. The federal government uses a chart that everyone follows. The chart shows how much money a person makes and what percentage of income he or she will pay in taxes. The more money someone makes, the higher the tax he or she pays.

Your First Job, Your First Tax Filing

You won't have to deal with paying taxes until you start to work. When you do find employment—whether it's a summer job, a part-time job, or a full-time job—you will start paying taxes on the money you earn. Employees usually have taxes taken out of, or withheld from, each paycheck. When you start a new job, your employer will ask you to provide information on a form called a W-4. This form helps your employer determine how much money to withhold from your wages and how much to pay to the government on your behalf. It is important to fill out your form accurately and completely. It is also very important to keep accurate financial records. When you file your taxes, you should keep your records in a safe location for at least seven years. Remember, you can be audited, or have your returns and records reviewed by the IRS, up to three years after you file a return. Should you ever be audited, having your past financial records and a copy of your tax forms handy is crucial.

State taxes are calculated in a number of ways. For those states that have an income tax, the tax is based on a percentage of your income. Sales tax, the tax paid when someone purchases items at a store, is a flat tax. That means everyone pays the same amount. For example, in New York City, most purchases are rung up with an additional 8.875 percent in state and city sales taxes. If you buy a CD for $10, the total cost of the CD will come to $10.89. The tax of eighty-nine cents is divided between the city and the state. The money is used for services offered to residents of New York City and New York State.

Sales tax is applied to many consumer products (food is usually exempt). Sales tax is a flat tax. Everyone in an area pays the same rate, which can vary greatly by state.

What is taxed as part of each state's sales tax varies by state. However, most states include the following: furniture, clothing, machinery and equipment, books, computers, boats, candy, cosmetics, cigarettes and tobacco, jewelry, art, collectibles, and

building materials. There are some items that are exempt from taxation in nearly all states. These exempt items include food, medicines and certain medical equipment, periodicals, and college textbooks.

Annually, the IRS conducts audits. A tax audit is an investigation into the tax documents filed by a person or corporation. Audits are used to ensure that tax documents are completed correctly and that all taxes that a person or corporation should be paying are actually submitted. A computer selects tax returns at random for auditing. Also, audits are done if the IRS detects unusual activity. On average, the IRS audits just one of every ninety-seven returns filed.

Taxpayers are also allowed exemptions and deductions. An exemption is an amount of money you can subtract from your income for being married and/or for having kids. Children are called dependents. Deductions are personal expenses that the government allows you to subtract from your income. These might include educational expenses, medical expenses, and business expenses, among others.

Keeping Taxes Fair

Some people pay more in taxes. Other people might use the services that taxes fund more than others. How do we keep taxes fair? There are two criteria used to measure fairness in taxes. The first is benefits received and the second is the ability to pay. Benefits received means that people should pay taxes in proportion to the benefits they receive in government goods and services. The ability to pay means that people's taxes should be in proportion to their resources.

Ways to File

You can file your tax return in one of two ways. You can file electronically using a computer, or you can fill out the forms by hand and mail them in using the U.S. Postal Service. There are key benefits to electronically preparing and filing your tax returns. These include increased accuracy, faster refunds, and the ability to file your federal and state returns simultaneously.

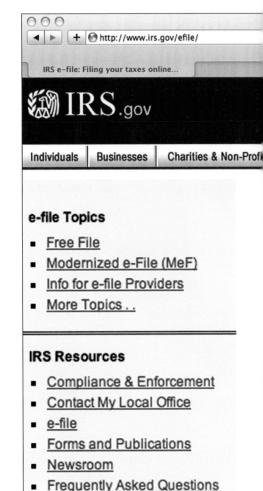

Tax filers can also fill out the forms themselves or hire a professional.

Completing the forms yourself often requires the use of tax preparation software and a personal computer. The software

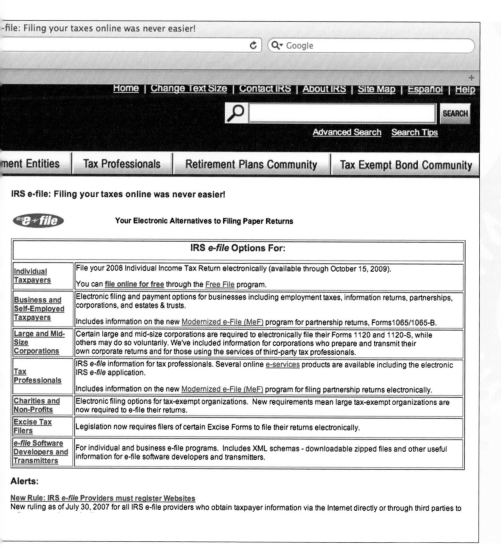

-file: Filing your taxes online was never easier!

Home | Change Text Size | Contact IRS | About IRS | Site Map | Español | Help

Advanced Search   Search Tips

ment Entities | Tax Professionals | Retirement Plans Community | Tax Exempt Bond Community

IRS e-file: Filing your taxes online was never easier!

irs e-file   Your Electronic Alternatives to Filing Paper Returns

IRS e-file Options For:	
Individual Taxpayers	File your 2008 Individual Income Tax Return electronically (available through October 15, 2009). You can file online for free through the Free File program.
Business and Self-Employed Taxpayers	Electronic filing and payment options for businesses including employment taxes, information returns, partnerships, corporations, and estates & trusts. Includes information on the new Modernized e-File (MeF) program for partnership returns, Forms 1065/1065-B.
Large and Mid-Size Corporations	Certain large and mid-size corporations are required to electronically file their Forms 1120 and 1120-S, while others may do so voluntarily. We've included information for corporations who prepare and transmit their own corporate returns and for those using the services of third-party tax professionals.
Tax Professionals	IRS e-file information for tax professionals. Several online e-services products are available including the electronic IRS e-file application. Includes information on the new Modernized e-File (MeF) program for filing partnership returns electronically.
Charities and Non-Profits	Electronic filing options for tax-exempt organizations. New requirements mean large tax-exempt organizations are now required to e-file their returns.
Excise Tax Filers	Legislation now requires filers of certain Excise Forms to file their returns electronically.
e-file Software Developers and Transmitters	For individual and business e-file programs. Includes XML schemas - downloadable zipped files and other useful information for e-file software developers and transmitters.

Alerts:

New Rule: IRS e-file Providers must register Websites
New ruling as of July 30, 2007 for all IRS e-file providers who obtain taxpayer information via the Internet directly or through third parties to

The Internal Revenue Service's Web site (http://www.irs.gov) offers valuable information to help in understanding federal and state taxes.

gives taxpayers access to the latest rules and regulations. Also, using a computer enables taxpayers to transmit their returns from home, the workplace, or a library.

Hiring a professional means giving a tax professional your tax information. The tax expert then calculates the information on your behalf. Tax professionals can include certified public accountants (CPAs), tax attorneys, IRS-enrolled agents, or tax preparation businesses. Tax professionals charge a fee for preparing your taxes.

Many people leave the task of completing tax forms to professional tax advisers or accountants when it is time to file their annual tax returns. Choosing the right person for the job is important. You should look for someone who is knowledgeable about your state's tax policies and who will support you if the IRS decides to select your tax documents for audit. The next page lists important questions to ask a tax adviser to better understand why we pay taxes, where the money goes, and how to file your returns.

Ten Great Questions
to Ask a Tax Adviser

1 Why do we pay taxes?

2 Why are there so many different types of taxes?

3 Where does our tax money go when it's collected?

4 What are my responsibilities as a taxpayer?

5 When do I file my tax return?

6 How do I file my tax return?

7 How are my taxes calculated?

8 What happens if I don't file a return?

9 What is a refund and how do I get one?

10 What happens if I am audited?

CHAPTER THREE
The History of Taxes

Taxation is an ancient system that can be traced back to the days of the pharaohs in Egypt and to the Roman Empire. Both civilizations collected taxes. These taxes were mostly imposed on goods that were imported into these countries, or exported out to neighboring countries.

Taxation in the United States dates back to colonial times and the earliest days of our country's history. In fact, taxes were one of the main reasons the American colonists fought for independence when our nation was a colony of England. Our tax system, which includes federal, state, and local taxes, has changed many times throughout our nation's history. There have been times when taxes have been raised to help pay for wars and times when taxes have been lowered to help build our economy. Some of the changes to our tax system can be traced directly to events, such as the Civil War, while other adjustments were made in response to changes in society or the economy.

Taxes, as we know them today, began when America was a colony of England. England needed to raise money to pay for its wars against France. This led England to impose taxes on the thirteen colonies. The Stamp Act of 1765 was the first tax imposed directly on the American colonies by England. The new tax required the American colonists to pay a tax on every piece of printed paper they used. This included everything from papers that accompanied shipments of goods to legal documents, licenses, newspapers, other publications, and even playing cards. This tax was troubling to the colonists for one reason: It was a measure imposed by England to raise money. Until the Stamp Act, taxes had only been used to regulate the economy.

The most famous protest of taxation by the American colonies was the Boston Tea Party. On December 16, 1773, after

The Boston Tea Party was a pivotal moment for the American colonies. After refusing to pay England's increased tax on tea and other imports, the colonists revolted by throwing tea overboard into Boston Harbor.

officials in Boston, Massachusetts, refused to return three shiploads of taxed tea to Britain, a group of colonists boarded the ships and destroyed the tea by throwing it into Boston Harbor. The American colonists fought against the Tea Act for a number of reasons, but mainly because they believed it violated their right to be taxed only by their own elected representatives.

No Taxation Without Representation

Even though colonists were forced to pay the tax the Stamp Act created, they were angry because they were financially supporting a government they had no say in running. This led to the rallying cry of the American Revolution: "Taxation without representation is tyranny."

As part of the American Revolution, in which America broke away from England and won independence, the country worked to create its own federal government. During this process, our Founding Fathers wrote the Declaration of Independence and the Articles of Confederation, which became the country's first constitution in 1781. A constitution provides a framework for the organization of a government. With the establishment of this new nation, the citizens of the United States now had proper democratic representation. However, this new government made no money of its own and relied on donations from its states to provide it with an income.

The U.S. Constitution replaced the Articles of Confederation in 1787. The document defined the three main branches of the government: the legislative branch, the executive branch, and the judicial branch. The legislative branch includes the House of Representatives and the Senate. Each state elected representatives to fill positions in the House and Senate, giving each state a voice in the federal government.

When the U.S. Constitution was being written, our Founding Fathers knew that our country would need to raise money to build cities, establish roads, and create a military for protection. They also realized that the government could not function properly if it relied entirely on its states for its resources. As a result, the federal government was granted the authority to raise money and impose taxes on the American people. The Constitution gave Congress the power to "lay and collect taxes, duties, imposts, and excises, pay the debts and provide for the common defense and general welfare of the United States."

Taxation Without Representation Today

The citizens of the District of Columbia (Washington, D.C.) do not have representation in the U.S. Senate. Washington, D.C., is a district and is not recognized as a full-fledged state. As a result, a campaign has grown over the years for the district to have a senator or congressperson represent its interests. In November 2000, the D.C. Department of Motor Vehicles began issuing license plates with the slogan "Taxation Without Representation." In a show of support for the city, President Bill Clinton used the "Taxation Without Representation" plates on the presidential limousine.

Funding a Growing Nation

As our country has grown and evolved since it first declared independence in 1776, so have our taxes. Our government has made adjustments to the tax system as circumstances have created the need for more money. War and times of growth and prosperity have influenced taxation.

The United States first raised money from tariffs, which were the largest source of federal revenue from the 1790s to the beginning of the Civil War, when income taxes were established. A tariff is a tax, or duty, imposed on goods when they are moved from one country to another. The goods cannot continue on their way until the tax is paid. When the Civil War began, the U.S. government needed more money to pay for the war. As a result, Congress passed the Revenue Act of 1861, which imposed a tax on personal income, or the money people made from working. This income tax was a new direction for our federal tax system, which until this time had been based mainly on excise taxes and tariffs. When it became clear that the Civil War would not end as quickly as the government thought it would, the federal government realized it would need more money. According to the Web site of the U.S. Department of the Treasury, Congress created new excise taxes on such items as gunpowder, feathers, telegrams, iron, leather, pianos, yachts, billiard tables, drugs, patent medicines, and whiskey. Many legal documents were also taxed, and license fees were collected for many professions.

After the Civil War ended, the government realized it didn't need as much money, so the income tax was abolished in 1872. The Spanish-American War in 1898 created a renewed need for money, so taxes were established on items such as beer,

The Civil War marked the first time the American government imposed a tax on personal income. In need of money to fund the war, the United States established the annual income tax in 1861.

tobacco, and gum. In 1913, the Sixteenth Amendment was approved. It allowed Congress to impose an income tax without dividing it among the states or basing it on the results of a census, which tracks the size of the population.

The United States' involvement in World War I greatly increased the need for revenue. Congress responded by passing the Revenue Act of 1916. The act doubled the lowest income tax rate from 1 percent to 2 percent and increased the top tax rate to 15 percent for those people who had incomes of more than $1.5 million. Our government was slowly realizing two problems: There was not an organized way to collect taxes, and not everyone paid their taxes. In 1918, only 5 percent of the population paid their income taxes, and yet it was this tax that was funding one-third of the cost of the war.

After the war came to an end, the economy boomed during the Roaring Twenties, a time in our country of social, artistic, and cultural growth. Increases in revenues from income taxes followed as people began to make

more money. The United States saw a huge growth in industry as new technologies, especially cars and movies, grew in popularity. Taxes were cut five times to encourage the growth of the economy. But all of this came crashing down on October 29,

After the stock market crash of 1929, the United States was thrust into the Great Depression. Many people pulled money out of banks. To improve its finances, the government raised taxes in the 1930s.

1929. Known as Black Tuesday, this was the day the stock market on Wall Street collapsed, plunging the country into economic despair. The event led to the Great Depression, when millions of people were out of work. People struggled to find jobs throughout much of the 1930s. As the economy shrank and people lost their jobs, there was less income to tax and the government felt the effects. Congress increased taxes to keep money coming into the government. The downside was that those who were lucky enough to have jobs saw a greater portion of their income go to the government. Also, many now believe that the tax increases further weakened the economy.

The Financial Costs of War

When World War II broke out, the United States needed money to fund its involvement in the war. It was a very tense time for tax policy in our country. Everyone from the president to congressmen agreed that taxes needed to be high to create revenue to pay for the supplies our soldiers needed. In 1940, only around 10 percent of the population paid federal income tax. By 1944, just four years later, nearly every employed person paid income taxes. This tax money went toward soldiers' salaries, goods they needed in combat, food to feed the troops, and equipment to support military efforts. World War II led to the creation of the Bureau of Internal Revenue, which later became the Internal Revenue Service (IRS). The IRS is the world's largest accounting and tax collection organization. The IRS created a "pay-as-you-go" system of tax withholding. In this system, taxes are withheld from each person's paycheck and sent to the government instead of individuals paying taxes in one lump sum each year.

Benefits of new tax law

The new tax law expands and provides new tax relief to help parents save and pay for their children's education. Some of the education provisions of the Economic Growth and Tax Relief Reconciliation Act of 2001:

Education IRAs

■ Expands annual contribution limit from $500 per child to $2,000 per child from birth through age 17

■ In 2002, Education IRAs established for children can also accept contributions from corporations, tax-exempt organizations and other entities

■ Can use Education IRA to pay for elementary and secondary tuition or expenses, regardless of whether the school is public or private

Higher education expenses deduction

■ Deduction for qualified higher education expenses; phases out after 2005

Student loan interest deduction

■ Deduction of student loan interest beyond the first 60 months in which interest payments are required

■ Deduction of voluntary interest payments, such as those made during forbearance period

Qualified tuition plans

■ Expands the scope of qualified tuition plans; no longer restricted to state-sponsored qualified tuition plans

■ Private colleges and universities also able to sponsor these types of programs

■ Changes tax treatment of withdrawals from tuition plans; able to withdraw the money tax-free if used to pay for qualified college expenses

Source: Dallas Morning News research
Graphic: Robert West, The Dallas Morning News

© 2001 KRT

The Economic Growth and Tax Relief Reconciliation Act of 2001 lowered tax rates and created educational savings incentives to help parents offset the rising costs of their children's college education.

While the pay-as-you-go system (which is still used today) made it easier for both the taxpayer and the tax collectors, it also reduced the taxpayer's knowledge of how much money is being collected. This made it easier for the government to raise taxes without taxpayers feeling the burden immediately.

Our government continued to make changes to our tax system as the country changed. In the 1980s, President Ronald Reagan drastically reduced taxes. His Economic Recovery Tax Act of 1981 reduced the amount of federal income tax for American workers. When many of the tax cuts the act created went into effect, the economy began a pattern of growth that lasted throughout much of the 1980s. The 1990s and 2000s saw a number of tax acts, from the Taxpayer Relief Act of 1997, which gave families a tax credit for each child in a family, to the Economic Growth and Tax Relief and Reconciliation Act of 2001, which cut taxes slightly.

Today, taxes continue to change and evolve as our government leaders look for ways to maintain or increase tax revenue while balancing the impact on the American worker. History has shown us that as our country enters wars and periods of economic growth and depression, and as the government needs more money to fund initiatives, taxes will continue to be raised and lowered to help support various projects.

CHAPTER FOUR
The Effects of Taxes

Taxes often influence what people buy and how much they feel they can spend on a particular item. If a tax raises the price of an item too high, a person may decide not to make a purchase. This is one of the effects taxes can have on people and their decisions.

Tax Changes

Our federal and state governments can change taxes as often as they want to. All that's needed is for a new tax bill to be passed in Congress. Sometimes the government raises taxes to help pay for war or a struggling economy. Other times, taxes may be lowered to help taxpayers keep more money in their pockets. Taxes often change from year to year. Tax increases and tax cuts are both very common.

To understand the effect of a tax increase, we need to take a look at who bears the burden of the tax. For example, suppose the price of a T-shirt is $10 and the government imposes on

T-shirt sellers a tax of 10 percent per T-shirt. A few weeks after the tax goes into effect, the tax causes the price of a T-shirt to increase to $11. The T-shirt sellers receive the same amount per T-shirt as they did before the tax, so the tax increase has not made the sellers worse off. Instead, consumers pay the entire tax in the form of higher prices. What if taxes are increased and instead of 10 percent per T-shirt the tax becomes 15 percent? That $10 T-shirt now costs $11.50. Would you buy it now that it costs more due to an increase in taxes? Now imagine how much more you would pay in taxes on items that cost thousands of dollars, like cars or boats.

A tax cut is a reduction in taxes. When a tax cut occurs, the government sees a decrease in the income it receives from taxes. Those who pay taxes see an increase in the amount of money they get to keep from their paycheck. Sometimes when taxpayers receive more money from a tax cut, they decide to spend it. This helps the economy grow. When people purchase more products, they pay more in local and state taxes, such as sales tax. But when the economy is bad and there is a tax cut, people tend to save any extra money they receive. This hurts the economy. While people have more money to spend, they are scared to spend it because they are unsure of what lies ahead. They think they might need that extra money in the future.

How Taxes Are Spent

When the federal government collects our taxes, it uses them to pay for expenses that keep our government running. Each year the federal government creates a budget and makes it available for citizens to see. You might be wondering what our government spends our tax dollars on. Below is a sampling of programs:

Social Security/Medicare: Retired people are eligible to collect Social Security once they reach a certain age. We each pay Social Security taxes to ensure that one day we will receive this money back to help support us as we age.

Defense: This covers everything from military salaries to wars in foreign countries to the research, development, and purchase of new technologies.

Low-income programs: Some of our taxes go toward programs that help those who cannot support themselves. These programs include food stamps, housing support, and childcare assistance.

Interest on the federal debt: The federal government has debt, and a lot of it. Taxes help us pay off the debt the government owes on loans.

Education: While states cover the majority of education costs, our government contributes to programs for low-income school districts, special education, and financial aid programs for college students.

Health research: Keeping our nation healthy is important. Our taxes fund the Food and Drug Administration (FDA) and dozens of programs that keep our citizens healthy.

Veterans' benefits: The federal government provides income and health benefits to people who have fought in wars or worked for our military.

Community development: In the event of a major natural disaster—such as Hurricane Katrina, which destroyed much of the city of New Orleans, Louisiana—the Federal

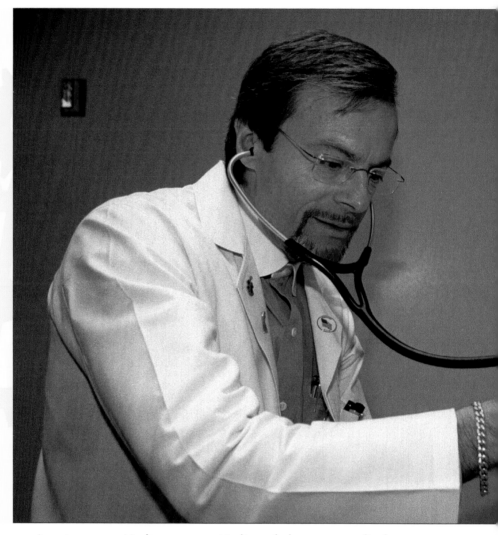

Americans pay Medicare taxes. Medicare helps cover medical expenses, treatments of illnesses, and regular checkups of seniors.

Emergency Management Agency (FEMA) assists people in rebuilding their lives and communities.

Highways/mass transit: Most highway and mass-transit spending is supported by the taxes we pay. This includes

roads, bridges, and bus and subway systems.

Prisons: Our taxes also support prisons and law enforcement programs.

Unemployment benefits: These programs temporarily provide benefits to people who are unable to find jobs.

International affairs: This includes the operation of American embassies abroad and contributions to organizations such as the United Nations.

Natural resources/environment: Taxes help fund national parks, federal lands, water projects, and environmental cleanup.

Agriculture: Farms may receive assistance from the government to be successful or to stay in operation.

The U.S. Federal Budget

The federal budget of the U.S. government is created by the president of the United States and is sent to the U. S. Congress at the beginning of the year, in January or February. Senators and Congress members make additional recommendations

Our taxes help support infrastructure projects in the greater community. These could include new bridges, highways, and subway tunnels, like this one in Pittsburgh, Pennsylvania.

after they review the budget, and then the budget is sent back to the president for approval. Once the president approves the budget, it goes into effect on October 1 each year. Certain parts of the budget are mandatory expenses, such as Social Security and Medicare. But other spending is flexible. The government must decide what to fund and what it may hold off on funding until the following year. Sometimes money is taken away from one area to support another. When the United States is at war, military spending increases, so cuts are made to other areas to help create a balanced budget and control overspending.

Can We Eliminate Taxes?

Getting rid of taxes altogether has been a proposed idea for some time. While people would earn more money and their purchasing ability would increase, federal and state governments wouldn't earn any income from taxation and couldn't pay for services that are shared by everyone.

Without taxes, our country might not have the money to defend itself against war or provide even the most basic of services. The government would not be able to function if we did not support the people who run it. Local services used by those in need (e.g., public assistance, police and firefighters) would need to be paid for by individuals, who could not afford them, and many services would simply disappear. There would be no maintenance on roads or bridges, and snow would not be removed in the winter months. If part of our country was struck by a natural disaster, no aid would be available to help the people in those communities rebuild.

Careers in the IRS

The Internal Revenue Service does more than just make sure you are paying your taxes. Since the IRS is a large federal agency, it has numerous career tracks to explore. While the IRS employs a number of accountants to check tax returns and answer questions when people need assistance in filing their tax documents, it also employs professionals with all sorts of professional backgrounds. The IRS hires lawyers, computer specialists, law enforcement agents, researchers and analysts, administrative people, and executives who participate in the highest level of decision making within the organization. To be hired by the IRS, you don't even need a background in math or accounting. The organization accepts applications from people with backgrounds in accounting, business, communications, information technology, computer science, law, research, and finance.

Tax Resistance

Refusing to pay your taxes as a matter of conscience is called tax resistance. Tax resisters decide they no longer want to pay taxes because they disagree with how tax revenues are being spent or feel tax rates are unfair. Some protest the idea of taxes, and others even refuse to pay in an attempt to damage or overthrow a government. Refusing to pay your taxes is a risky thing to do and can result in penalties that include high fines and possibly time in jail or prison.

Richard Hatch, a winner of CBS's *Survivor*, failed to pay taxes on the $1 million he won on the reality TV show. Hatch was sentenced to prison for tax evasion.

Tax evasion is when people use illegal means to avoid paying taxes they owe. Failing to file a tax return, failing to report all of one's income, or concealing income earned illegally (through gambling, theft, etc.) are all forms of tax evasion. Tax evasion is a serious crime and brings with it serious penalties. The IRS can fine a person for evading taxes. The fine includes the amount the person owes the government, plus a penalty amount that can total thousands of dollars. The IRS can also send you to prison for up to one year for every year you avoided filing your tax return.

MYTHS and FACTS

MYTH You cannot be audited once you have received your refund.

FACT Receiving your refund just means the IRS has reviewed your tax return and agreed with your calculations. That doesn't mean it won't go back to check that your filing is complete and accurate. Also, if the IRS receives a return from a separate party who names you and that information does not match your return, you can be audited. The IRS can audit a return up to three years after it is received.

MYTH Students are exempt from filing tax returns.

FACT Many people believe that being a student means they don't have to file a tax return or pay their taxes. But it's untrue. Students must pay taxes on their income and file a tax return. Students do get special tax credits for being a student and can deduct some of their educational expenses, which may lower their tax bill.

MYTH My tax preparer or accountant is liable for mistakes on my tax forms.

FACT The only person responsible for your tax documents is you, no matter who prepared them. Many taxpayers believe that if they use a professional accountant, that person is held responsible for any errors or omissions. Even if your accountant made a mistake, you will still need to pay for it.

CHAPTER FIVE
The Future of Taxes

Not everyone agrees that we should pay taxes. In fact, there have been many attempts throughout history to protest or end taxation. While these protests have gotten some results, they have not ended the need for taxes, nor have they provided another way for our government to earn money to pay for services that we all use and need. The way we pay taxes might change in the future, but we will likely always pay taxes in some form.

One of the first protests against taxation was the Boston Tea Party. On December 16, 1773, after officials in Boston refused to return three shiploads of taxed tea to Britain, a group of colonists boarded the ships and destroyed the tea by throwing it into Boston Harbor. The colonists objected to the Tea Act because they believed it violated their rights. Many colonists believed they should be taxed only by representatives they elected themselves, and not by a distant government like the British Parliament. The event led to the Revolutionary War; however, it did not end taxation. The reality is that citizens need

Since colonial times, when taxes were first imposed to finance the government, there have been arguments in America about the fairness of taxes.

to pay taxes so that the government can function and provide for its people.

There have been other proposed tax plans that could replace the federal and state income taxes we pay. One such idea is the Fair Tax Plan, which would replace all federal income tax with a single, national retail sales tax. Instead of paying taxes on the money you earn from your job, you would pay a higher sales tax on all items you buy. Proponents of the plan say that there could be many positive outcomes from this new tax plan, among them:

- Federal income taxes would no longer exist.
- Financially challenged individuals would no longer be taxed, giving them more money.
- Current government services would continue to be supported because the money raised from a national sales tax would be equal to the amount of revenue earned from the federal income tax.
- People might feel that they have more control over how much they spend in taxes. Because the Fair Tax Plan is based on what consumers buy, people could exercise a certain amount of control over how much tax they paid by purchasing less.
- It would be much harder to avoid paying taxes. Since the current tax system is voluntary and relies on people to file their own tax returns, there are people who avoid paying taxes each year.

But with every new idea there are negative aspects as well. Opponents say that less positive outcomes of the Fair Tax Plan could be:

- The price of goods and services would increase.
- If the income tax is not fully abolished, a future president and/or representatives could reinstate part of the federal income tax program in response to a national emergency or crisis. This could result in Americans paying both a higher national sales tax and a federal income tax.
- The plan could make it easier for the government to raise the tax rate on certain items that it deems unhealthy or dangerous, such as cigarettes, firearms, or junk food.

Facts About the U.S. Tax System

The U.S. tax system is an amazing system that supports our nation and everyone living within its boundaries. When looking at the system's history, there are details that surprise most Americans, such as the fact that we started paying annual federal income taxes only in 1913. Back then, paying taxes wasn't as easy as having the money taken out of paychecks. Paying taxes annually required people to save money in anticipation of paying a lump sum to the federal government. It wasn't until World War II, when the government needed a steady stream of income to fund the war, that taxes were withheld from paychecks. This practice continues today. The American tax code has since become a complex system. Some say that it is the biggest, most complicated document ever assembled. Our tax code has more than seven million words and keeps increasing. Comparatively, the Bible only has about seven hundred thousand words.

- The plan could cause an increase in crime. If the tax rate is too high, it could cause people to steal needed items and sell them for profit.

Changing the Way Taxation Works

Changing the way taxes work is called tax reform. Tax reformers, or the people who want to make the changes, are interested in changing the way taxes are collected and managed, reducing the amount of taxes people pay, and making the tax system easier to understand. Today, people try to reform or change the tax system by passing new laws. However, one of the first tax change efforts ever attempted was the Whiskey Rebellion of 1794, which turned violent.

The Whiskey Rebellion occurred when President George Washington decided to tax whiskey to help pay off the country's national debt. Farmers thought the tax was unfair because they normally converted their excess grain into liquor as part of their livelihood. Also, it taxed the farmers for making whiskey, but not the people who bought it. Tensions grew out of control as farmers and other supporters protested and attacked tax collectors. Washington sent 12,950 troops to western Pennsylvania, near Pittsburgh, to put an end to the rebellion.

The Whiskey Rebellion is just one of the many events in history in which the American people have tried to reform the tax system. As new ideas have been introduced, some guiding principles on how to judge tax reform proposals have been developed. First, new tax systems should be simple so that taxpayers can understand the amount of taxes they are paying. Also,

Steve Forbes, a Republican presidential candidate in 1996 and 2000, supported a flat income tax, or the same tax rate for everyone. His ideas were controversial, and he lost his bid for election during the primaries.

they should clearly instruct people on how to pay their taxes and offer deadlines and easy ways to make payments. New tax systems should be fair to the poor, the middle class, and the wealthy. Finally, it should be clear to people what is being taxed (income, property, purchases) and at what rate or percentage.

The truth is, even though there will always be new proposals for how to collect taxes, we need to pay taxes to help our government operate efficiently.

A Tax-Free Society

What would our country be like if we paid no taxes? Can we live in a tax-free society? There have been organizations and groups that have suggested that we end the current taxation system and adopt a tax-free society. These groups have suggested many ways to create this system. One proposal is for every person to donate a certain amount of money to a trust fund. A trust fund is an account to which money is added and the interest is paid to the party named on the trust. In this case, the American people would donate

money to a trust, and the government would receive money from the trust to support the operation of the government.

Suppose we lived in a society without taxation. If there were no taxes, the government would not earn any income from

The Cayman Islands do not impose income or property taxes on citizens. Instead, the Caribbean nation raises money through import and export taxes, tourist fees, work permit fees, and transaction fees.

taxation and citizens would not spend their hard-earned money on taxes. If someone had a wage of $10 an hour, he or she would be able to keep the entire amount. Many people in support of a society without taxation think that if taxation did not exist, people would spend more money. Maybe they would even work harder, knowing that they could keep every cent they earned.

What about the opposite situation? What if taxes were 100 percent of your income? In other words, every cent of what you earned would go to the government. If you didn't get to keep any of the money you earned, would you work? Most likely, you would not. What would be the point?

There are a few countries that have tax-free societies. The Cayman Islands, located in the Caribbean Sea, do not impose income or property taxes. The country's government raises money through taxes placed on importing and exporting goods and on fees charged to tourists, work permit fees, and transaction fees. This may be an extreme example, but it shows us how society could operate in such a scenario.

Our Taxation System

As American citizens, we all share the same freedoms. Since we all partake of the benefits that this affords us, we should contribute to making our country the best place to live. Taxes give us that opportunity.

While there are many different systems of taxation in the world, every one of them has its pros and cons. It may not be a perfect system, but the U.S. government has stuck to this current tax system because it works.

GLOSSARY

audit A review of your tax return by the IRS, during which you may be asked to prove that you have correctly reported your income, deductions, and exemptions.

debt Something that is owed, such as money, goods, or services.

deduction An expense you are permitted to subtract from your taxable income before figuring your tax bill.

dependent Someone you support and for whom you can claim a dependency exemption on your tax return.

electronic filing Filing your tax documents online. It is the fastest way to get your tax return to the IRS (and your state's revenue office).

exemption An amount of income exempted from taxation. Taxpayers can claim a personal exemption for themselves and for a spouse. Taxpayers can also claim an exemption for a child or other dependent.

FICA The Federal Insurance Contributions Act tax, which pays for Social Security and Medicare.

import tax A tax imposed on goods when they are moved across a political boundary.

income The amount of money you earn.

lawmaker A person who writes and passes laws.

parliament The legislative body of Great Britain, which has the power to pass and amend laws.

progressive tax A tax in which the tax rate increases as the taxable amount increases.

rebellion An organized refusal to obey certain laws.

revenue The income of a government from taxes and other sources.

sales tax A tax charged at the point of purchase for certain goods and services.

tax bracket A division by which the amount of income taxes you pay are defined.

tax evasion Avoiding taxes intentionally, and by using illegal tactics.

tax reform The process of changing the way taxes are organized, collected, and managed by the government.

tax return A document filed by a taxpayer that gives the government an outline of what he or she owes in taxes for a given year.

veteran A person who has served in the armed forces.

withholding The amount held back from your paycheck that is used to pay your income and Social Security taxes.

FOR MORE INFORMATION

Americans for Fair Taxation
P.O. Box 27487
Houston, TX 77227-7487
(713) 963-9023
Web site: http://www.fairtax.org
Americans for Fair Taxation is a nonprofit organization
   dedicated to replacing the United States' current tax
   system. The group has proposed the FairTax plan as
   an alternative.

Canadian Tax Foundation
595 Bay Street
Suite 1200
Toronto, ON M5G 2N5
Canada
(416) 599-0283
Web site: http://www.ctf.ca
The CTA strives to improve the understanding of the
   Canadian tax system.

Council on State Taxation
122 C Street NW
Suite 330

Washington, DC 20001
(202) 484-5222
Web site: http://www.cost.org
The Council on State Taxation is a state tax organization
   representing taxpayers.

Institute for Professionals in Taxation
600 Northpark Town Center
1200 Abernathy Road, Suite L-2
Atlanta, GA 30328-1040
(404) 240-2300
Web site: http://www.ipt.org
This professional organization is for those employed in
   the field of taxation.

Internal Revenue Service
500 N. Capitol Street NW
Washington, DC 20221
(202) 874-6748
Web site: http://www.irs.gov
The Internal Revenue Service is the nation's tax
   collection agency.

National Tax Association
725 15th Street NW #600
Washington DC 20005-2109
(202) 737-3325
Web site: http://www.ntanet.org
The NTA is an association of tax professionals dedicated to
   advancing the understanding of public finance.

Tax Foundation
National Press Building
529 14th Street NW
Suite 420
Washington, DC 20045-1000
(202) 464-6200
Web site: http://www.taxfoundation.org
The mission of the Tax Foundation is to educate taxpayers
    about sound tax policy and the size of the tax burden borne
    by Americans at all levels of government.

Web Sites

Due to the changing nature of Internet links, Rosen Publishing
has developed an online list of Web sites related to the subject
of this book. This site is updated regularly. Please use this link
to access the list:

http://www.rosenlinks.com/rwe/taxa

FOR FURTHER READING

Bedeksy, Baron. *What Are Taxes?* (Economics in Action). New York, NY: Crabtree Publishing Company, 2008.

Bochner, Arthur, Rose Bochner, and Adriane G. Berg. *The New Totally Awesome Money Book for Kids*. New York, NY: Newmarket Press, 2007.

Bodnar, Janet. *Raising Money Smart Kids: What They Need to Know About Money and How to Tell Them*. New York, NY: Kaplan Business, 2005.

De Capua, Sarah. *Paying Taxes* (True Books: Civics). San Francisco, CA: Children's Press, 2002.

Foote, Tracy. *The Kid's ROTH IRA Handbook: Securing Tax-Free Wealth from a Child's First Paycheck or Money Answers for Employed Children, Their Parents, the Self-Employed and Entrepreneurs*. Indianapolis, IN: TracyTrends, 2008.

Giesecke, Ernestine. *Your Money at Work: Taxes.* (Everyday Economics). Portsmouth, NH: Heinemann Library, 2003.

Harmon, Hollis Page. *Money Sense for Kids*. Hauppauge, NY: Barron's Educational Series, 2005.

Holmberg, Joshua. *The Teen's Guide to Personal Finance: Basic Concepts in Personal Finance Every Teen Should Know*. Bloomington, IN: iUniverse, 2008.

Kishel, Ann-Marie. *Government Services*. Bel Air, CA: Lerner Classroom, 2007.

Kishel, Ann-Marie. *What Is Government?* Bel Air, CA: Lerner Classroom, 2007.

Kowalski, Kathiann M. *Taxes* (Open for Debate). Salt Lake City, UT: Benchmark Books, 2005.

Larsen, Kirsten. *Tara Pays Up!* (Social Studies Connects). New York, NY: Kane Press, 2006.

Loewen, Nancy. *Taxes, Taxes!: Where the Money Goes* (Money Matters). Mankato, MN: Picture Window Books, 2005.

Minden, Cecilia. *Understanding Taxes* (Real World Math). Ann Arbor, MI: Cherry Lake Publishing, 2009.

Orr, Tamra. *A Kid's Guide to Earning Money*. Hockessin, DE: Mitchell Lane Publishers, 2008.

BIBLIOGRAPHY

American Institute of Certified Public Accountants. "Understanding Tax Reform: A Guide to 21st Century Alternatives." AICPA.org, October 17, 2005. Retrieved August 11, 2009 (http://tax.aicpa.org/ Resources/Tax+Advocacy+for+Members/Tax+ Legislation+and+Policy/Understanding+Tax+Reform+ A+Guide+to+21st+Century+Alternatives.htm).

Anthony, Joseph. "7 Tips for Hiring a Tax Pro." Retrieved August 12, 2009 (http://businessonmain.msn.com/ knowledgeexchange/articles/adaptingandgrow.aspx? cp-documentid=18964878).

Boortz, Neal, and John Linder. "The Fair Tax Book: Saying Goodbye to the Income Tax and the IRS." New York, NY: Harper Paperbacks, 2006.

Cayman.com. "Benefits of Living in a Tax Free Country." October 9, 2008. Retrieved August 8, 2009 (http:// cayman.com.ky/about-cayman/financial-services/ benefits-living-in-tax-free-country.html).

Colonial Williamsburg. "A Summary of the 1765 Stamp Act." History.org. Retrieved August 11, 2009 (http://www. history.org/history/teaching/tchcrsta.cfm).

Huddleston, Cameron. "Five Steps to Hiring a Tax Pro." January 2009. Retrieved August 9, 2009 (http://www.

kiplinger.com/features/archives/2007/02/
    taxpro.html?kipad_id=49_).
Internal Revenue Service. "Understanding Taxes." IRS.gov.
    Retrieved August 10, 2009 (http://www.irs.gov/app/
    understandingTaxes/student/index.jsp).
Karlonia blog. "Fair Tax Pros and Cons." Karlonia.com,
    April 16, 2007. Retrieved August 11, 2009 (http://www.
    karlonia.com/2007/04/16/fair-tax-pros-and-cons).
Kaufman, Wendy. "Random Tax Audits Return to the
    IRS." October 9, 2007. Retrieved August 11, 2009
    (http://www.npr.org/templates/story/story.php?
    storyId=15111003).
McCormally, Kevin. "Don't Worry About an Audit."
    March 21, 2008. Retrieved August 14, 2009
    (http://www.kiplinger.com/columns/taxtips/archive/
    2006/tax0216.html).
Parrish, Geov. "Why Pay Taxes?" April 3, 2006. Retrieved
    August 11, 2009 (http://www.commondreams.org/
    views06/0403-27.htm).
PBS. "How Does Government Affect Me?" PBS.org.
    Retrieved August 12, 2009 (http://pbskids.org/
    democracy/govandme).
Retirement Living Information Center. "Taxes by State."
    RetirementLiving.com. Retrieved August 10, 2009
    (http://www.retirementliving.com/RLtaxes.html).
Saching.com. "Importance of Taxes: Why Should We Pay
    Tax to the Government?" June 18, 2009. Retrieved
    August 11, 2009 (http://www.saching.com/Article/
    Importance-of-taxes--Why-should-we-pay-tax-to-the-
    government/2682).

Schnepper, Jeff. "5 Tax Myths That Can Cost You Money."
July 6, 2009. Retrieved August 8, 2009 (http://articles.
moneycentral.msn.com/Taxes/AvoidAnAudit/
5taxMythsThatCanCostYouMoney.aspx).

Schoen, John W. "How the Government Spends Your Taxes."
MSNBC.com, April 3, 2008. Retrieved August 2, 2009
(http://www.msnbc.msn.com/id/23924282).

Tax World. "A History of Taxation." Taxworld.org. Retrieved
August 12, 2009 (http://www.taxworld.org/History/
TaxHistory.htm).

TeenAnalyst. "Introduction to Taxes." TeenAnalyst.com.
Retrieved August 13, 2009 (http://www.teenanalyst.
com/taxes/introtaxes.html).

TeenAnalyst. "Types of Taxes." TeenAnalyst.com. Retrieved
August 10, 2009 (http://www.teenanalyst.com/taxes/
varioustaxes.html).

U.S. Department of the Treasury. "History of the U.S. Tax
System." Retrieved August 11, 2009 (http://www.treas.
gov/education/fact-sheets/taxes/ustax.shtml).

INDEX

A

Agriculture, Department of, 21
alcohol, taxes on, 18, 40
American Revolution, 38
April 15 deadline, 25
Articles of Confederation, 38
audits, 26, 29, 31, 34, 35, 57

B

Black Tuesday, 44
Boston Tea Party, 37–38, 58
Bureau of Internal Revenue, 44

C

certified public accountants
      (CPAs), 34
cigarettes, 18, 30, 61
Civil War, 36, 40
corporate taxes, 12

D

Declaration of Independence, 38
deductions, 31, 57
dependents, 31
direct taxes, 18
District of Columbia, 39

E

Economic Growth and Tax
      Relief and Reconciliation
      Act of 2001, 46
Economic Recovery Tax of
      1981, 46
Education, Department of, 21
electronic filing, 32–34
Environmental Protection Agency
      (EPA), 21
excise taxes, 12, 18, 19, 40
exemptions, 31

F

Fair Tax Plan, 60
Federal Emergency Management
      Agency (FEMA), 50
Federal Insurance Contributions
      Act, (FICA), 14
flat taxes, 16, 29
food, taxes on, 16, 19, 31, 61
Food and Drug Administration
      (FDA), 49
food stamps, 23, 49
Founding Fathers, 7, 10,
      38, 39

G

gambling, 18, 56
Great Depression, 44

H

Health and Human Services,
    Department of, 21
Housing and Urban
    Development,
    Department of, 21
Hurricane Katrina, 49

I

import taxes, 67
income taxes, 5, 12–14, 19, 23,
    25, 29, 40, 42, 44, 46, 60,
    61, 64, 66
indirect taxes, 19
Internal Revenue Service (IRS),
    20, 25, 26, 29, 31, 34,
    44, 54, 56, 57

J

joint filing, 13

L

Labor, Department of, 21
luxury taxes, 18

M

Medicaid, 5, 21, 22
Medicare, 5, 21, 22, 49, 53

N

National Aeronautics and
    Space Administration
    (NASA), 21
national debt, 49, 62

P

pay-as-you-go system, 44, 46
progressive taxes, 13
property taxes, 12, 16–17, 19,
    64, 66

R

Reagan, Ronald, 46
refunds, 25, 32, 35, 57
Revenue Act of 1861, 40
Revenue Act of 1916, 42
Revolutionary War, 58

S

sales taxes, 12, 15–16, 19, 29,
    30, 48, 60, 61, 64
sin taxes, 18
Social Security, 5, 12, 14, 21, 23,
    49, 53
Spanish-American War, 40
Stamp Act of 1765, 37

T

tariffs, 40
tax advisor, ten great questions
    to ask a, 35

"taxation without representation," 38, 39
taxes
    effects of, 47–56
    future of, 58–66
    history of, 10, 36–46
    myths and facts about, 57
    obesity and, 19
    understanding, 4–7, 8–22
    why we pay, 23–34, 35
tax evasion, 25–26, 56
Taxpayer Relief Act of 1997, 46
tax reform, 62, 64
tax resistance, 54, 56
Tea Act, 38, 58
Treasury, Department of, 40
trust funds, 64–65

U

unemployment, 14, 51
United Nations, 51
U.S. Congress, 19, 39, 40, 42, 44, 47, 51
U.S. Constitution, 10, 38–39
U.S. Postal Service, 10, 32

W

Wall Street, 44
Washington, George, 62
W-4 forms, 29
Whiskey Rebellion of 1794, 62
withholding, 5, 29, 61
World War I, 42
World War II, 44, 61

About the Author

Laura La Bella is a writer and editor living in Rochester, New York. Among her books, La Bella has profiled actress and activist Angelina Jolie in *Celebrity Activists: Angelina Jolie Goodwill Ambassador to the UN*; has reported on the declining availability of the world's fresh water supply in *Not Enough to Drink: Pollution, Drought, and Tainted Water Supplies*; and has examined the food industry in *Safety and the Food Supply*.

Photo Credits

Designer: Sam Zavieh; Editor: Andrea Sclarow; Photo Researcher: Marty Levick